Plains

The Hidatsa, the Mandan, and the Arikara people shared a similar culture (permanent agricultural settlements versus nomadic, temporary settlements). They were united as one tribe but had a number of villages along the Missouri River. Like-a-Fishhook Village was one such village.

Permanent summer villages of the Hidatsa, Mandan, and Arikara people

United States forts

Temporary villages of the Crow and Lakota, who moved to follow the buffalo

Rivers

State and national borders (North Dakota became a state in 1889 and Montana in 1890.)

Fort Berthold

Like-a-Fishhook Village

Big Hidatsa Village

Fort Clark

Mandan Village

HIDATSA

MANDAN

ARIKARA

Arikara Village

Fort Lincoln

Knife River

Heart River

On-A-Slant Mandan Village

Missouri River

LAKOTA

This earth is alive and has a soul or spirit, just as you have a spirit. Other things also have spirits, the sun, clouds, trees, beasts, birds.

—Missouri River, Buffalo Bird Girl's grandfather

Buffalo Bird Girl

A Hidatsa Story

RETOLD BY S. D. NELSON

Abrams Books for Young Readers · New York

"I was born in an earth lodge by the mouth of the Knife River, in what is now North Dakota, three years after the smallpox winter."

A Hidatsa mother and child photographed around 1908. Buffalo Bird Girl would have been carried by her mother and aunts in a similar way.

My name is Buffalo Bird Woman, *Waheenee*, and my people are known as the Hidatsa. When I was young, they called me Buffalo Bird Girl—after the little brown bird that lives on the prairies of the Great Plains. This name has brought me fortune, for buffalo have a strong heart and the birds of the air have a good spirit.

In my life I have seen beautiful things and I have lived through hard times. When I was six years old, a terrible sickness called smallpox set upon my people with a fury. The cruel disease first appeared on the Great Plains many years before my birth. It arrived with the coming of the white men. They did not bring the sickness on purpose, but Indians could not fight off this disease—they had no immunity to the dreaded evil spirit.

Smallpox passed some by, but, sadly, it took the lives of many Hidatsa people, including my mother, my brother, and one of my aunts. My grandmother and two aunts survived. They raised me with the same love and kindness as my real mother.

We lived in a village of earth-mound lodges on the high bluffs of the Missouri River. We called it Like-a-Fishhook Village, for it was built upon a sharp bend. One side of our settlement was protected by the mighty river. The other side faced the vast, open prairie and was fenced off with stout posts: a stockade for protection from enemy tribes. The aggressive Lakota Indians, in particular, were constantly trying to steal our horses, our supplies of corn, and other belongings.

Our village was the home of two different Indian tribes: the Hidatsa and the Mandan. We had formed an alliance in order to increase our strength in numbers so we would be less vulnerable to attack. Like-a-Fishhook Village was the center of much activity, with people constantly coming and going.

"It was cool inside, never hot and stuffy."

My family's earth-mound lodge was large, measuring more than forty feet in diameter. It needed to be, for it was home to my father, grandmother, brothers and sisters, cousins, and uncles and aunts—twelve people in all. Inside, four enormous cottonwood posts stood like trees. They supported timber crossbeams that carried the great weight of packed earth. There was a fire pit in the center, with a smoke hole in the roof above.

In the shadows beyond the four posts were more columns. They held the log rafters and the leaning walls. Various household items and baskets of dried corn and squash hung from poles set across the rafters. Bed frames ringed the interior. Each served as a bed as well as a place to sit. The bedposts were draped with old tipi coverings for privacy; this canopy also kept out drafts. At night, everyone slept on buffalo robes.

OPPOSITE: *A reconstruction of an earth-mound lodge at On-A-Slant Indian Village, Fort Abraham Lincoln State Park, Mandan, North Dakota. Outside the lodge is a drying stage, accessed by a ladder cut from a single tree.*

ABOVE AND LEFT: *Inside the reconstructed lodge, massive tree posts hold up the timber crossbeams that in turn carry the great weight of the earth that covers the lodge. The smoke hole in the roof allows light to enter and hearth smoke to escape.*

A woman pounds corn into meal in a corn mortar in the manner Buffalo Bird Girl would have learned. Photographed in 1914.

For three seasons of the year, this is where we lived, and I considered it my permanent home. Here I learned many of the duties expected of a Hidatsa woman.

Work began early every day. I remember awaking to the comforting sound of a crackling morning fire. My grandmother and aunts would already be awake, preparing breakfast. I learned by watching and then by doing. A favorite breakfast for us children was hot corn porridge. To make it, Grandmother would pound hard kernels of corn into a fine meal in a wooden mortar. She boiled dried squash and beans in a clay pot filled with river water. Then she added the cornmeal mixed with roasted buffalo fat to the pot of vegetables. It tasted delicious! We women and girls always ate in a separate area from the men and boys.

Just like Buffalo Bird Girl's grandmother, a woman uses a bone hoe, made from a buffalo shoulder blade, to turn up soil and weeds in a row of squash. Photographed in 1912.

In the spring, when green buds appeared on the gooseberry bushes, we knew the time for planting had arrived. Families from each earth lodge had their own garden. The women and girls did the farming. We planted corn, squash, beans, and sunflowers in the rich soil of the lowlands nearby. There were several varieties of corn: yellow, white, and red. We used digging sticks and iron hoes to loosen the earth and get rid of weeds. My grandmother used a hoe made of bone from a buffalo shoulder blade attached to a stick.

"We thought that the corn plants had souls, as children have souls."

From spring to harvest, my younger sister and I would sit atop a platform, keeping careful watch over our cornfields. Hungry crows, gophers, and horses were a constant threat. They needed to be chased away. Prowling boys from the village liked to sneak among the rows of corn, too, and steal cobs! We would yell their names when we saw them and threaten to tell their mothers.

Corn plants have a spirit, as do all living things. Even clouds, stars, and the rocks of the earth are a part of the one Great Spirit. We girls who kept watch often sang songs to the corn. We sang in the same way a mother sings to her young child. We believed the corn plants enjoyed listening to our songs.

The men did the hunting. They sought buffalo, antelope, deer, and other large animals. The boys hunted small animals, such as rabbits, and birds, such as grouse and ducks.

Removing the hides, or skinning, was a task we all shared. The women would prepare and cook the fresh meat for everyone to enjoy. They would slice up the remaining meat and dry it on racks outdoors. Rising smoke from a fire helped cure and preserve the meat so it would last a long time.

The women also scraped and tanned the animal hides. They used the prepared skins to make clothing and tipis. Like other tribes on the prairies, we needed tipis whenever we traveled. The women even made the bull boats used for river travel, out of bent willow saplings and rawhide.

All of these things I learned by watching and then doing.

Fort Berthold, where Buffalo Bird Girl and her family and fellow villagers went to trade goods. Photographed in 1865.

Friendly tribes such as the Crow and Shoshone regularly visited our village. They traded horses for our corn. White fur traders came into our country, too, seeking animal furs, especially buffalo hides. For these, they would trade us supplies that we desired. They built a trading post near our village and called it Fort Berthold. It was exciting to see steamboats come upriver and unload items to trade. To us the white man's goods—kettles, guns, metal knives, iron hoes, and sugar—were wonderful new luxuries.

Sometimes I was allowed to go into the fort. There I would see colored glass beads, metal cooking pots, and colored fabric, as well as the different people: missionaries, settlers, gold seekers, and soldiers. Their strange hats and clothing with buttons seemed marvelous. Even the language they spoke while bartering was a curiosity.

Hidatsa and Mandan men began hunting buffalo for trade. They killed more than I imagined possible. At the trading post, buffalo hides were heaped in piles like mountains. We received goods such as metal tools, rope, and coffee, and the men were given liquor. We were told that the hides were sent downriver, then back east to be processed into leather goods.

"I look back upon my girlhood as the happiest time of my life."

In our farming community there was often extra time for fun. The boys played games that tested physical skill: They shot arrows, wrestled, and raced horses. We girls were not allowed to play with the boys. Instead, we played house with dolls, kickball, and my favorite game, hide-toss.

In hide-toss, a group of girls held on to the edges of a large buffalo hide and used it to take turns tossing one another into the air. The goal was to see who could fly the highest while standing and keep her balance the longest. Show-offs would twist from side to side as they bounced in the air, turning a full circle in two bounds. I could hardly wait for my turn. I would fly as high as the others and flutter-kick my feet. At the height of each bounce, my stomach would feel as if it were turning upside down. We would shriek and laugh until we were exhausted.

A twentieth-century Hidatsa doll similar to one that Buffalo Bird Girl and her friends might have had. These dolls were meant for play and were not used in ceremonies.

During the summer season we picked ripe berries and dug prairie turnips. The gathering of firewood needed to be done year-round. The job was less difficult with the help of our family dogs. My dog's name was Shee-peesha, or Blackie. I raised him from a puppy and remember wrapping him in a blanket and carrying him on my back the way a mother carries her baby. When he was old enough and strong enough, he joined the other family dogs in hauling firewood.

Just as my grandmother had taught me, I rigged my dog with a harness, two long poles, and a cross-frame called a travois. We had to travel quite some distance with our dogs in order to reach the wooded areas along the river. Men would accompany us to watch for enemies. Once there, we chopped dry tree limbs and driftwood with iron-head hatchets. We tied armloads of firewood on our dog's travois (but never more than a strong dog could pull). Often, upon returning, I would reward Shee-peesha with an extra chunk of meat.

LEFT: *This woman holds a string of prairie turnips. Buffalo Bird Girl and other girls and women of her village would gather wild vegetables and fruits from the prairies. If not eaten fresh, the vegetables and fruits were dried and stored for winter use. Photographed in 1916.*

BELOW: *Prairie turnips*

> *"Suddenly there came a sound, poh-poh-poh, as of guns . . . and a woman screamed."*

One summer, the Lakota attacked in broad daylight! Thirty mounted men came yelping over the ridge. *Poh-poh-poh*—they fired their guns. The horse thieves had come for more than just corn; they wanted slave women and children, too! My sister and I shrieked as we ran from our platform in our cornfield. Other women and children ran crying toward the village.

A painted Lakota horseman with an eagle-feather headdress galloped along the edge of our cornfield. A young Hidatsa guard named Red Hand was ready and charged his horse to meet the enemy. The Lakota launched an arrow into the air. The shaft struck Red Hand's horse in the neck, and it fell beneath him. But brave Red Hand landed on his feet. He raised his rifle, took steady aim, and fired. Immediately, the Lakota brute slumped forward and dropped his bow. His pony turned in retreat.

Yelping Hidatsa and Mandan warriors seemed to appear from everywhere to repulse the attack. The Lakota quickly realized they were greatly outnumbered. They had no choice but to flee. Our warriors gave chase.

After nightfall our men returned. They rode into the village, triumphant victors with war stories and the scalp of one unfortunate Lakota. As was the custom, our women built a great fire for the celebration. Everyone painted their faces black and joined in the traditional scalp dance. It was a joyous party that lasted late into the night.

RIGHT: *In a manner similar to Buffalo Bird Girl and her people, a woman skewers squash slices on a spit. Photographed in 1916.*

BELOW: *A man rests beneath a drying stage where the slices of squash, strung on spits, have been laid to dry in the sun. Photographed in 1916.*

"And then came the corn harvest, busiest and happiest time of all the year."

With the attack behind us, the women and girls had to attend to harvesting the crops. First we gathered the squash. We sliced each vegetable into sections, pierced them with rods or spits, and hung them on racks in the sun to dry.

The corn, which had ripened on the stalks, was ready for harvesting next. (Later we would gather the beans and sunflower seeds.) The women and girls from each lodge collected their ears of corn in baskets and heaped them near the center of their individual gardens. There was so much corn that the men and boys would help with the husking. We peeled back the husks and braided the corn together into bundles. Each bundle of braided corn held about fifty ears and was heavy.

After the harvest, Buffalo Bird Girl would have helped hang the braided ears of corn and spread the loose ears on a corn stage as depicted in this photograph from 1909.

The bundles were hung on the rails of a framework known as the drying stage. Small ears of husked corn were not braided together. Instead, people carried them in baskets to the drying stage and spread them to cure in the sun. The corn had to be completely dry before being placed in storage; otherwise, it would spoil.

The women and older girls separated the dried kernels from the small, loose cobs in a process called threshing. The threshing was done in a tent beneath the drying stage. The women beat the corn with sticks, knocking the kernels from the cobs. The walls of the tent kept the flying kernels from bouncing away.

Then we gathered the beans and sunflower seeds. After the harvest, in preparation for the next year's crop, the women set aside plenty of extra ears of corn. The best kernels from these cobs would be the seeds for next spring's planting. We saved the ripest and best-colored seeds from our squash, beans, and sunflowers as well.

LEFT: *A ladder descends into a storage cache inside an earth-mound lodge. In the background is a platform used as both a bed and a place to sit. These platforms would line the outer edge of the lodge.*

RIGHT: *Buffalo Bird Girl would have used a similar basket to carry the dried vegetables to the cache.*

We hung some of the bundles of braided corn in the family lodge for immediate use. We also kept some sacks of threshed corn. But much of our dried corn, squash, and beans was stored in underground chambers called caches.

My grandmother taught me how to use a buffalo shoulder blade like a shovel to hollow out an underground cavity. The pit would be deeper than a man is tall; a ladder was needed to climb in and out. We would line the walls with dry grass and then fill the pit with corn and other dried crops. When the cache was full, the opening was covered with dry grass and hidden beneath dirt. Robbers would have a hard time finding the buried treasure!

The contents could be dug up whenever needed. Some caches were dug into the floor of the lodges, but most were outdoors. In this way dried corn, beans, and squash lasted throughout the winter. We had plenty to eat when the prairies were covered in snow.

"With a little ochre and buffalo fat, I painted my cheeks a bright red."

As the days grew shorter and the nights turned cold, I could actually smell the change of seasons. The cottonwood trees transformed from green into gold. A successful harvest meant giving thanks to the Great Spirit and celebrating. On such occasions, I would wear my finest beaded dress. We women and girls would braid our hair and apply makeup to our faces. At night, drumming and singing rose from the village. We all took our turn at dancing, many with painted faces and in handsome costumes. The scene was magnificent! Men and women always danced separately. Likewise, boys and girls did not dance together.

This girl of the Kiowa tribe wears a tanned leather dress similar to what Buffalo Bird Girl and other Hidatsa girls would have worn on special occasions. On the dress are woven cowrie shells and elk teeth. Photographed in 1895.

"We all wore winter moccasins, fur lined, with high tops."

Winter on the Great Plains can be merciless. For this reason, my people did not live upon the exposed banks of the Missouri River year-round. The river iced over and remained frozen like rock for months. With the onset of the cold winter months, we vacated Like-a-Fishhook Village and moved to the wooded lowlands. Everyone in the village packed up the stores of food and other belongings. We lashed everything in bundles onto travois, which were pulled by horses and dogs. The bottomlands were thick with trees and offered some protection from the brutal blizzards that howled across the prairie. There was also a better supply of firewood. Each winter we selected a new location to build our temporary winter lodges. When our food supplies ran low, some of our people returned to Like-a-Fishhook Village to gather corn and dried vegetables we had buried in the storage caches. This way we were never hungry.

An 1838 engraving of an Ohio River steamboat. Vessels such as this would stop at Fort Berthold and its trading post on the Missouri River, bringing goods as well as many white soldiers, adventurers, and eventually settlers.

"And so I grew up, a happy, contented Indian girl."

With the end of each winter, the sun traveled higher in the sky and warmed the earth. The thick ice on the Missouri River began to thaw and break up. Migrating geese flew northward in great waves that filled the sky. Their thrilling song assured us that spring was coming. All of the Hidatsa and Mandan people knew then that it was time to return to Like-a-Fishhook Village.

Our world was constantly changing. Raids from the warring Lakota tribe continued. Steamboats arrived frequently during the summer, bringing more white men to our village. Another tribe, known as the Arikara, decided they could not survive alone; smallpox and the warring Lakota had taken too many of their lives. We welcomed them into Like-a-Fishhook Village. In spite of the outside pressures, we continued to live close to our Mother Earth and to follow her ways—we watched and listened for the changing of the seasons.

"I am an old woman now. The buffaloes and black-tail deer are gone, and our Indian ways are almost gone. Sometimes I find it hard to believe that I ever lived them."

Buffalo Bird Woman. This photograph was taken in 1910 after she and the other villagers had been moved to the Fort Berthold Indian Reservation.

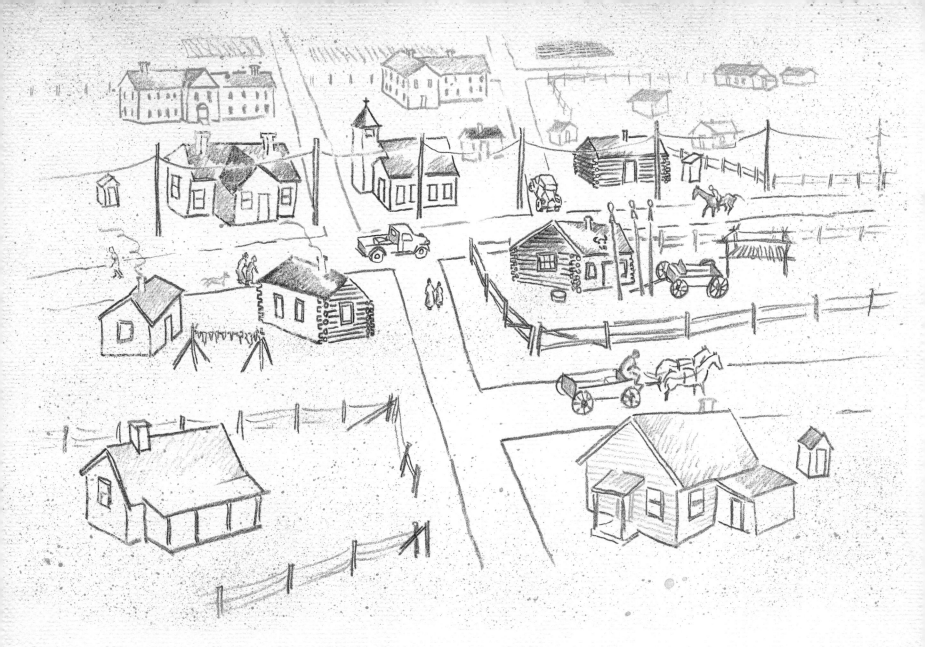

Like-a-Fishhook Village is gone now. There are no buffalo left to hunt, and the fur trade ended long ago. The government of the United States said my people had to move from our village. They promised to provide rations of food and clothing if we lived on a reservation. The government built roads, schools, and churches. They told us that our children had to learn to live the white man's way. So we Hidatsa, as well as the Mandan and Arikara people, gave up our round earth lodges and began living in square cabins on the Fort Berthold Indian Reservation.

"But I have not forgotten our old ways. . . .
In the shadows I seem again to see our Indian village,
with smoke curling upward from the earth lodges."

With the passing of winter, the days grow warm. Green buds appear on the gooseberry bushes—signaling the arrival of spring and the time for planting. Not far from my square house, there is open space for a garden. The seeds that have been carefully stored through the long winter are brought forth. My old hands can still loosen the earth with a hoe and set kernels in the black soil. Inside each seed sleeps the spirit of life, waiting to sprout.

In my memories of long ago, I hear two girls singing—my sister and I. We are singing to the corn in the same way a loving mother sings to her child. And in the moist earth, unseen, there comes a gentle stirring of new life.

Author's Note

MY STORY

As a boy living in North Dakota, one of my favorite meals was my Lakota mother's corn soup. My mother maintained many traditional ways: She cut thin slices of beef and hung them on racks to dry. Along with my Euro-American father, she planted a garden every spring. Corn, squash, and beans were always essentials. In late summer she would gather sweet corn, remove the kernels from the cobs, and dry the kernels on flats in the sun. Likewise, she would cut squash into strips and dry them. Months later, in the middle of winter, she boiled a delicious soup—my favorite!—using these ingredients. With her, we kids gathered chokecherries in late summer and mashed them into a pulp to make cherry syrup. My mother also made *wasna* (pemmican—pounded dried meat mashed together with tallow) and *wojapi* (berries mashed together with sugar and cornstarch). In autumn we all would gather wild ripe plums.

Like Buffalo Bird Girl, we also dug wild turnips in midsummer on the Dakota prairies. Sometimes we would use a traditional digging stick like hers. (Frankly, a steel-headed shovel really worked the best!) The turnips were braided into hanks and hung to dry. They kept throughout the winter and added a special earthy flavor to the corn soup.

AN INDIAN GIRL'S STORY

Buffalo Bird Woman, Waheenee-wea, was among the very last of the Hidatsa to live in the old ways of her people. With her hair turning gray, she grew concerned that the customs of the Hidatsa were vanishing and would be forgotten. Fortunately, in 1906, she was introduced to Gilbert Wilson. It seems destiny had called these two people together: Wilson, an anthropologist, had traveled westward seeking to record any vestiges of traditional life among Plains Indians. With a generous heart, Buffalo Bird Woman shared the fascinating details of her youth. Wilson wrote down everything he was told. Their collaboration resulted in the publication of remarkable stories, the hallmarks of which include *Buffalo Bird Woman's Garden* and *Waheenee: An Indian Girl's Story; Told by Herself to Gilbert Wilson.*

THE HIDATSA STORY

By the year 1100 CE, the Mandan people had established several farming communities along the upper reaches of the Missouri River in what is present-day North Dakota. The Hidatsa followed. By 1500, the two distinct tribes, with different languages and customs, lived as neighbors. Their total population numbered in the thousands. In the late 1700s and then again in the early 1800s, smallpox struck, with devastating results. At the same time, their enemy, the fierce Lakota, made constant war with them. In the 1840s, weakened and vulnerable, the Hidatsa and Mandan consolidated and escaped northward, where they established Like-a-Fishhook Village. Later they were joined by the Arikara, whose numbers had also diminished for similar reasons.

Most of the other tribes that lived on the Great Plains were hunters and gatherers. They hunted buffalo, deer, antelope, and other game. Likewise, they gathered prairie turnips, berries, plums, and other wild edible plants. Each tribe was unique, with names like Crow, Lakota/Sioux, Cheyenne, and Assiniboine. All of them were nomads (wanderers) who lived in tipis. Their primary source of food was the buffalo, or bison, which constantly moved in search of forage. The nomads followed the great herds entirely on foot. Interestingly, the wandering people did possess one domesticated animal: the dog. It was an animal they depended upon when they moved from one encampment to another. When rigged with a travois, the average dog could drag approximately thirty pounds of supplies and other belongings. Dogs even dragged the long poles used for supporting tipis.

The Hidatsa, Mandan, and Arikara, however, were both hunters and farmers. They often made forays onto the Great Plains, where they hunted game. But unlike the nomads, they lived in established settlements. Archaeologists call this way of life the "Plains Village Tradition." The Indians became renowned for their success as farmers. They cultivated corn, beans, squash, and sunflowers. In fact, the Hidatsa and Mandan grew a considerable surplus of crops that they stored as a food source to be used during the long winters on the Great Plains.

The surplus of agricultural foods created a burgeoning trade system for the Plains Village people. The nomadic tribes regularly visited the Hidatsa and Mandan to trade meat, leather goods, and other useful wares for dry corn, dry squash, and the like. This trading network expanded with the coming of the Euro-Americans.

The Traditional Way

The Hidatsa lived as close to the natural world as is humanly possible. Their earth-mound lodges, made from dirt and timbers, became part of the earth itself. All of their tools and weapons were made from stone, bone, wood, animal skins, and other natural materials. Every aspect of their existence was bound to the chang-

ing seasons and the fundamental ways of Mother Earth. The Hidatsa believed that everything in the natural world has a spirit: four-legged creatures, winged beings, green growing things, little creepy-crawlies, and we two-legged beings. Even the stars, the clouds, the rivers, and the stones of the earth had a soul. Everything in creation was interconnected and part of the Great Spirit.

Women and men had distinct roles; some of these gender-specific duties and expectations are explained in this story. These roles provided cohesion in the family and larger community.

At the heart of the natural world, there is both beauty and conflict. The Hidatsa sought to live in accord with this fundamental paradox. At times they intended to live in peace with their neighbors. But let there be no doubt: The Hidatsa were a warrior society. The men gained respect and status by demonstrating fierceness in battle. They protected their people from the Lakota and other enemy tribes who regularly raided their villages. Sometimes Hidatsa men initiated attacks and rode against the Lakota! Like their enemy, they admired a man who could prove his cunning and courage by successfully stealing horses and striking or killing an enemy. As a result, a state of constant conflict existed between the Hidatsa and the Lakota.

Clash of Cultures

When the Euro-Americans appeared on the Great Plains, they brought permanent changes for all Native Americans. In 1541, traveling north from Mexico, the Spanish conquistadors made contact with tribes on the southern Great Plains. They brought horses that, in time, would forever change the lives of all Plains Indians. Pierre Gaultier de Varennes, sieur de La Vérendrye, a French trader from Canada, first visited the Mandan villages in 1738 (there is no confirmed documentation that he encountered the Hidatsa, who lived nearby). Later, other fur traders followed, and by the 1780s, they had established sustained contact with all the horticultural tribes on the Missouri River.

Some changes were positive. New curiosities were introduced—metal tools, glass beads, guns, horses, cloth, and so much more. Others would eventually have a very negative effect, such as alcohol. Unintentionally, white traders brought germs and illnesses—such as smallpox, cholera, and measles—against which the Indians had no natural immunity. Smallpox is a particularly vicious disease. It attacks the human body with a terrible fever; vomiting follows, and then painful blisters appear in the mouth and throat and cover the body. Two-thirds of the Hidatsa died from smallpox alone. More than 80 percent of the Mandan perished.

By the late 1800s, all Native American people were forced by the U.S. government to move onto Indian reservations. In 1934, following the Indian Reorganization Act, the Hidatsa, the Mandan, and the Arikara officially united as the Three Affiliated Tribes on the Fort Berthold Indian Reservation, in North Dakota.

Today and the Future

The Hidatsa people are still here, as are the Mandan and the Arikara. They remain one sovereign nation. Each member of the nation has the same freedoms as every citizen of the United States. Like all other human beings, they face the many challenges of a rapidly changing world. Today they govern themselves with self-determination. Their words and actions give shape to their lives and hope for their children.

Acknowledgments

I wish to thank Buffalo Bird Woman for providing such rich stories about her Hidatsa way of life. Her complete story takes the reader from childhood to old age. I have chosen to focus on her childhood experience. Therefore, I have taken a few liberties, using episodes and examples of the Hidatsa traditions in this story that were actually explained during the narration about her adult life.

I would like to thank the staff at the Knife River Indian Villages National Historic Site, in Stanton, North Dakota, for their informative visitor center—in particular ranger Dorothy C. Cook, who gave me a personal tour of their reconstructed Hidatsa earth lodge. Also, I am grateful to the staff at Fort Abraham Lincoln State Park, North Dakota. The park, with its several reconstructed Mandan earth lodges, is a hidden treasure. Tracy Potter, the director of the Fort Abraham Lincoln Foundation, North Dakota, was most generous in sharing his knowledge about the Hidatsa, Mandan, and Arikara cultures.

Select Timeline

5000–3500 BCE: Indian farmers in Mesoamerica (the area extending from present-day mid-Mexico to Belize) cultivate maize/corn, beans, and squash.

200–900 CE: Corn is introduced by Mesoamerican peoples to the Indian tribes of North America through trade and migration (squash and beans arrive later).

1100s: Native Americans settle along the Missouri River in present-day North Dakota. They build villages of rectangular earth lodges and start farming.

1500s: Native Americans (ancestors of the Hidatsa and Mandan) build large round earth lodges upon the bluffs of the Missouri River. The size of their villages and cornfields increases. Unlike other nomadic tribes (Lakota/Sioux, Cheyenne, Blackfeet, and Comanche), they adopt a seminomadic lifestyle called the Plains Village Tradition.

1541: The Spanish conquistador Francisco Vásquez de Coronado explores present-day Kansas on horseback. Leading his expedition from Mexico, he is the first European to encounter American Indians on the southern Great Plains. It is also the first time Indians have ever seen a horse. Thereafter, the horse becomes a prized trade item among the Native Americans and a "vehicle" that will change their way of life.

1600s: The Hidatsa and Mandan villages have become the hub of a trading network with other tribes on the Great Plains. These nomadic tribes regularly visit to trade horses, meat, and fur for agricultural products.

1691–1700s: French, British, and Spanish fur traders are the first white men to make contact with the Native American inhabitants of the northern Great Plains. In exchange for animal furs, Indians receive horses, guns, glass beads, metal implements, liquor, and cloth. Diseases such as smallpox and measles are unintentionally passed to Indians with devastating results.

1738: Pierre Gaultier de Varennes, sieur de La Vérendrye, the French Canadian merchant-trader, travels to the Mandan villages on the Heart River and Missouri River.

Mid-1770s: White traders take up residence with the Mandan and Hidatsa. They intermarry and learn the customs and language of the Indians.

1781: The Mandan, Hidatsa, and Shoshoni tribes are devastated by smallpox.

1803: The Louisiana Purchase: The United States buys the vast expanse of land from the Mississippi River to the Rocky Mountains. Spain and France had previously claimed it from the Indians.

1804: Meriwether Lewis and William Clark lead the Corps of Discovery into the newly acquired land, where they meet eleven of the fourteen tribes that inhabit the area. They spend the entire winter encamped near the Mandan and also visit the Hidatsa. Their written account provides a detailed description of the Indian way of life.

1831: The steamboat *Yellow Stone* travels up the Missouri River. Many steamboats follow, creating an explosion in river travel and a boom in the fur trade business.

1832: George Catlin, artist and author, visits the Mandan and Hidatsa, who live together at a place called the Five Villages on the banks of the Knife River where it joins the Missouri River. He provides a detailed written account along with hundreds of drawings and paintings.

1833–34: The Swiss artist Karl Bodmer and the German ethnologist Prince Maximilian of Wied-Neuwied spend the winter at Fort Clark near the Mandan and Hidatsa villages on the Knife River. They observe and record Native American customs and ways of life in great detail. Bodmer creates scores of paintings that are considered by scholars to be among the finest illustrations of North American Indians.

1834: The Lakota/Sioux attack and burn two of the Hidatsa villages.

1837: The steamboat *St. Peter's* docks at Fort Clark, near the Hidatsa and Mandan villages on the Knife River. Passengers infected with smallpox unintentionally transmit the disease. Approximately seven-eighths of the Mandan population perishes. More than half of the Hidatsa people die.

1839–40: Buffalo Bird Girl is born in an earth lodge of the Hidatsa tribe along the Knife River in present-day North Dakota.

1845: Weakened by the smallpox epidemic of 1837 and vulnerable to attack, the Hidatsa and Mandan people join forces and move thirty miles north of the Knife River. United, these two tribes establish Like-a-Fishhook Village on the Missouri River, North Dakota.
The Fort Berthold trading post is built next to Like-a-Fishhook Village.
Smallpox strikes the Hidatsa winter village. Buffalo Bird Girl's mother, brother, and one aunt die.

1845: Manifest Destiny is declared to be a divine right by John L. O'Sullivan. He writes that it is "our manifest destiny to overspread the continent allotted by Providence for the free development of our yearly multiplying millions."

1862: The weakened Arikara tribe joins the Hidatsa and Mandan at Like-a-Fishhook Village.

1864: A military post is established at Fort Berthold by the U.S. government.

1870: The Fort Berthold Indian Reservation is created in present-day North Dakota. Eventually the reservation is reduced in size and today consists of 988,000 acres. It is home to the Three Affiliated Tribes: the Mandan, Arikara, and Hidatsa people.

1875: U.S. general Philip Sheridan states that by exterminating all the remaining buffalo herds the Indians will be deprived of their primary food source ("For the sake of lasting peace, let them [hunters] kill, skin and sell until the buffaloes are exterminated"). Originally, there were thirty million buffalo on the Great Plains. Within twenty years, they are nearly all extinct; only a few hundred remain on the entire continent.

1880s: The U.S. government moves the people of Like-a-Fishhook Village to the Fort Berthold Indian Reservation in North Dakota.

1906: Gilbert L. Wilson visits the Fort Berthold Indian Reservation and meets Buffalo Bird Woman. They will collaborate on two books: *Buffalo Bird Woman's Garden* and *Waheenee: An Indian Girl's Story.*

1932: Buffalo Bird Woman dies on the Fort Berthold Indian Reservation.

1934: The Indian Reorganization Act: The Hidatsa, Mandan, and Arikara officially unite as the Three Affiliated Tribes on the Fort Berthold Indian Reservation.

1956: The U.S. Army Corps of Engineers builds a great two-mile-long earthen dam blocking the flow of the Missouri River. Garrison Dam is built for flood control and for generating electricity. The remains of Like-a-Fishhook Village disappear beneath the man-made lake (Sakakawea Reservoir). The government floods 152,360 acres and relocates 90 percent of the people to higher ground. The Three Affiliated Tribes are paid $12.5 million in compensation.

2009: The Tribal Council approves the leasing of land for oil and gas drilling on the Fort Berthold Indian Reservation, which sits on top of the Bakken Shale Oil Formation. It is America's most promising oil and gas field, with estimated reserves of nearly four billion barrels of oil. To date, the Three Affiliated Tribes have received almost $180 million in payments.

Notes

Except epigraph, all quotes are by Buffalo Bird Girl and are from *Waheenee: An Indian Girl's Story; Told by Herself to Gilbert L. Wilson*; first published by Webb Publishing Company, Saint Paul, Minnesota, in 1921, and reprinted by the University of Nebraska Press (UNP) in Lincoln, in 1981. The page number at the conclusion of each entry below refers to the UNP 1981 paperback edition.

Epigraph: "This earth is alive and has a soul or spirit, just as you have a spirit. Other things also have spirits, the sun, clouds, trees, beasts, birds." Quote attributed to Missouri River, Buffalo Bird Girl's grandfather, 63.
Page 2: "I was born in an earth lodge . . . three years after the smallpox winter," 7.
Page 6: "It was cool inside, never hot and stuffy," 55.
Page 13: "We thought that the corn plants had souls, as children have souls," 94.
Page 19: "I look back upon my girlhood as the happiest time of my life," 54.
Page 22: "Suddenly there came a sound, *poh-poh-poh*, as of guns . . . and a woman screamed," 114.
Page 27: "And then came the corn harvest, busiest and happiest time of all the year," 109.

Page 33: "With a little ochre and buffalo fat, I painted my cheeks a bright red," 147.
Page 35: "We all wore winter moccasins, fur lined, with high tops," 129.
Page 36: "And so I grew up, a happy, contented Indian girl," 117.
Page 38: "I am an old woman now. The buffaloes and black-tail deer are gone, and our Indian ways are almost gone. Sometimes I find it hard to believe that I ever lived them," 180.
Page 40: "But I have not forgotten our old ways," adaptation of original quote: "I cannot forget our old ways," 175. "In the shadows I seem again to see our Indian village, with smoke curling upward from the earth lodges," 176.

Select Bibliography

Ambrose, Stephen E., and Sam Abell. *Lewis & Clark: Voyage of Discovery.* Washington, D.C.: National Geographic, 2002.

Bowers, Alfred W. *Hidatsa Social and Ceremonial Organization.* Washington, D.C.: U.S. Government Printing Office, Smithsonian Institution, 1965.

Catlin, George. *Letters and Notes on the North American Indians.* North Dighton, MA: J.G. Press Inc., 1995.

Diamond, Jared. *Guns, Germs, and Steel: The Fates of Human Societies.* New York: W. W. Norton & Company, Inc., 1997.

Gilman, Carolyn. *Lewis and Clark: Across the Divide.* Saint Louis: Missouri Historical Society Press; Washington, D.C.: Smithsonian Institution, 2003.

Gilman, Carolyn and Mary Jane Schneider. *The Way to Independence: Memories of a Hidatsa Indian Family, 1840–1920.* Saint Paul: Minnesota Historical Society, 1987.

Maximilian, Prince of Wied and Karl Bodmer. *Travels in the Interior of North America During the Years 1832–1834.* Cologne, Germany: Taschen, 2001.

Peters, Virginia Bergman. *Women of the Earth Lodges: Tribal Life on the Plains.* Oklahoma City: University of Oklahoma Press, 2000.

Potter, Tracy. *Sheheke, Mandan Indian Diplomat: The Story of White Coyote, Thomas Jefferson, and Lewis and Clark.* Helena, MT: Fárcountry Press; Washburn, ND: Fort Mandan Press, 2003.

Preston, Richard. "Demon in the Freezer," *New Yorker,* July 7, 1999.

Schneider, Mary Jane. *The Hidatsa.* New York: Chelsea House Publishers, 1989.

Taylor, Colin F. *The Plains Indians: A Cultural and Historical View of the North American Plains Tribes of the Pre-Reservation Period.* New York: Crescent Books, 1994.

———. *Sun'ka Wakan, Sacred Horses of the Plains Indians: Ethos and Regalia.* Wyk auf Föhr (Germany): Verlag für Amerikanistik, 1995.

———. *Yupika, The Plains Indian Woman's Dress: An Overview of Historical Developments and Styles.* Wyk auf Föhr, Germany: Verlag für Amerikanistik, 1997.

Trimble, Michael K. *An Ethnohistorical Interpretation of the Spread of Smallpox in the Northern Plains Utilizing Concepts of Disease Ecology.* Lincoln, NE: J & L Reprint Company, 1986.

Weatherford, Jack M. *Indian Givers: How the Indians of the Americas Transformed the World.* New York: Fawcett Columbine, 1988.

Wilson, Gilbert L. *Buffalo Bird Woman's Garden: Agriculture of the Hidatsa Indians.* Saint Paul: Minnesota Historical Society Press, 1917.

———. *Waheenee: An Indian Girl's Story; Told by Herself to Gilbert L. Wilson.* Saint Paul, MN: Webb Publishing Company, 1921; Lincoln: University of Nebraska Press, 1981.

Image Credits

Page 3: Library of Congress; Page 6: S. D. Nelson; Page 7: S. D. Nelson; Page 8: Minnesota Historical Society; Page 10: Minnesota Historical Society; Page 16: Smithsonian Institution, National Anthropological Archives; Page 19: S. D. Nelson; Page 21: State Historical Society of North Dakota 1952-5100, State Historical Society of North Dakota 0086-0391; Page 26: Minnesota Historical Society; Page 28: Image # 286444, American Museum of Natural History, Library; Page 31: S. D. Nelson; Page 33: National Museum of the American Indian, Smithsonian Institution (P13149); Page 36: Library of Congress; Page 38: Minnesota Historical Society

Index

Note: Page numbers in *italics* refer to illustrations.

For Robin Runs Strong

The paintings in this book were created with acrylic paint on gessoed Masonite. The drawings were made with black colored pencil on 140 lb. cold-press 100-percent-cotton acid-free paper.

Library of Congress Cataloging-in-Publication Data

Nelson, S. D.
Buffalo Bird Girl / by S. D. Nelson.
p. cm.
Includes bibliographical references and index.
ISBN 978-1-4197-0355-3
1. Hidatsa women—Biography—Juvenile literature. 2. Blind women—Biography—Juvenile literature. 3. Hidatsa Indians—Social life and customs—Juvenile literature. I. Title.
E99.H6N45 2012
978.4004'975274—dc23
2011035636

Text and original illustrations copyright © 2012 S. D. Nelson
Book design by Maria T. Middleton

Printed and bound in China
10 9 8 7 6 5 4 3 2 1

THE ART OF BOOKS SINCE 1949
115 West 18th Street
New York, NY 10011
www.abramsbooks.com

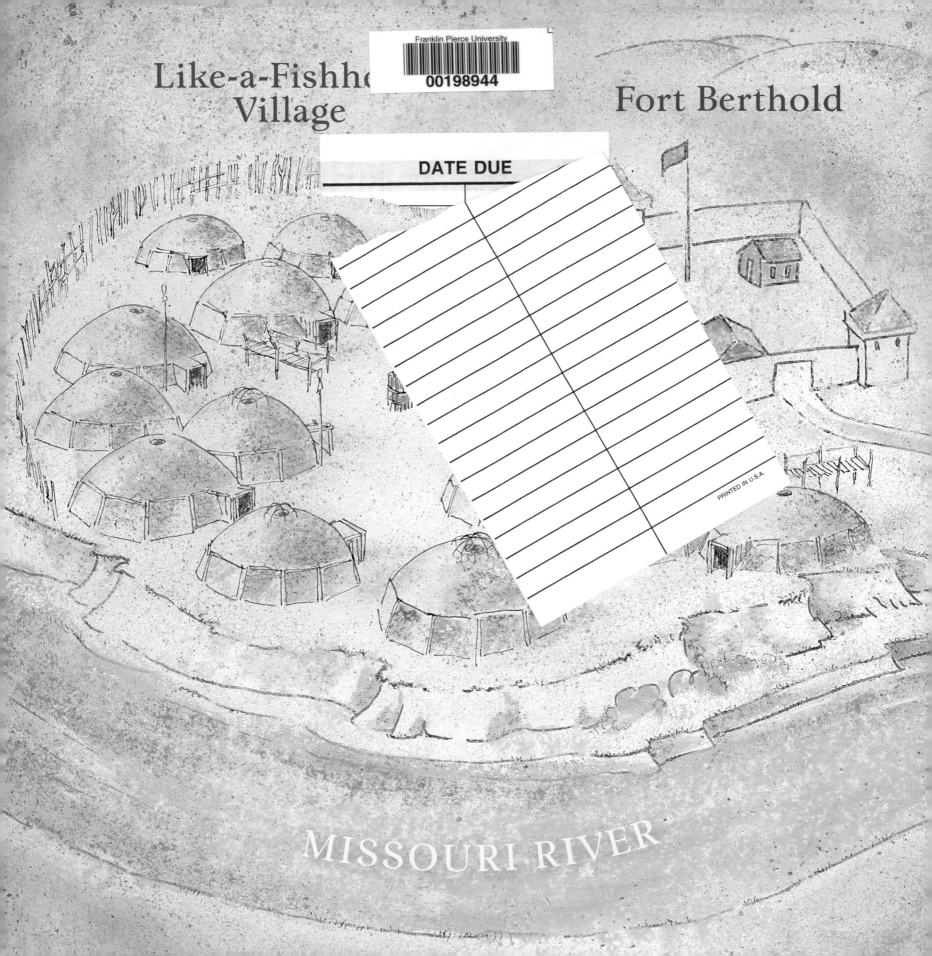